Too Much For Duck

and

The Wet Day

Maverick
Early Readers

'Too Much For Duck' and 'The Wet Day'
An original concept by Kate Poels
© Kate Poels 2023

Illustrated by Camilla Frescura

Published by MAVERICK ARTS PUBLISHING LTD
Studio 11, City Business Centre, 6 Brighton Road,
Horsham, West Sussex, RH13 5BB
© Maverick Arts Publishing Limited August 2023
+44 (0)1403 256941

A CIP catalogue record for this book is available at the British Library.

ISBN 978-1-84886-978-3

Maverick publishing
www.maverickbooks.co.uk

This book is rated as: Red Band (Guided Reading)
It follows the requirements for Phase 2/3 phonics.
Most words are decodable, and any non-decodable words are familiar, supported by the context and/or represented in the artwork.

Too Much For Duck
and
The Wet Day

By Kate Poels

Illustrated by Camilla Frescura

The Letter I

Trace the lower and upper case letter with a finger. Sound out the letter.

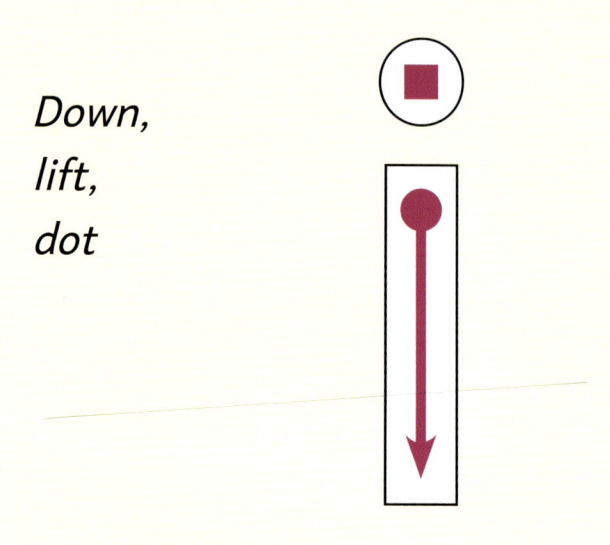

*Down,
lift,
dot*

*Down,
lift,
across,
lift,
across*

Some words to familiarise:

crowded   pond   rocks

High-frequency words:

it   was   in   the   said   is   no

Tips for Reading 'Too Much For Duck'

- Practise the words listed above before reading the story.

- If the reader struggles with any of the other words, ask them to look for sounds they know in the word. Encourage them to sound out the words and help them read the words if necessary.

- After reading the story, ask the reader why Duck hid.

Fun Activity

Discuss what you can do if something feels too much for you.

Too Much For Duck

It was too crowded in the pond.

It was too much for Duck.

Duck hid in the mud.

But it was still
too much for Duck.

Duck hid in the rocks.

But it was still
too much for Duck.

"This is too much!" said Duck.

"Yes," said Fish.
"This is too much."

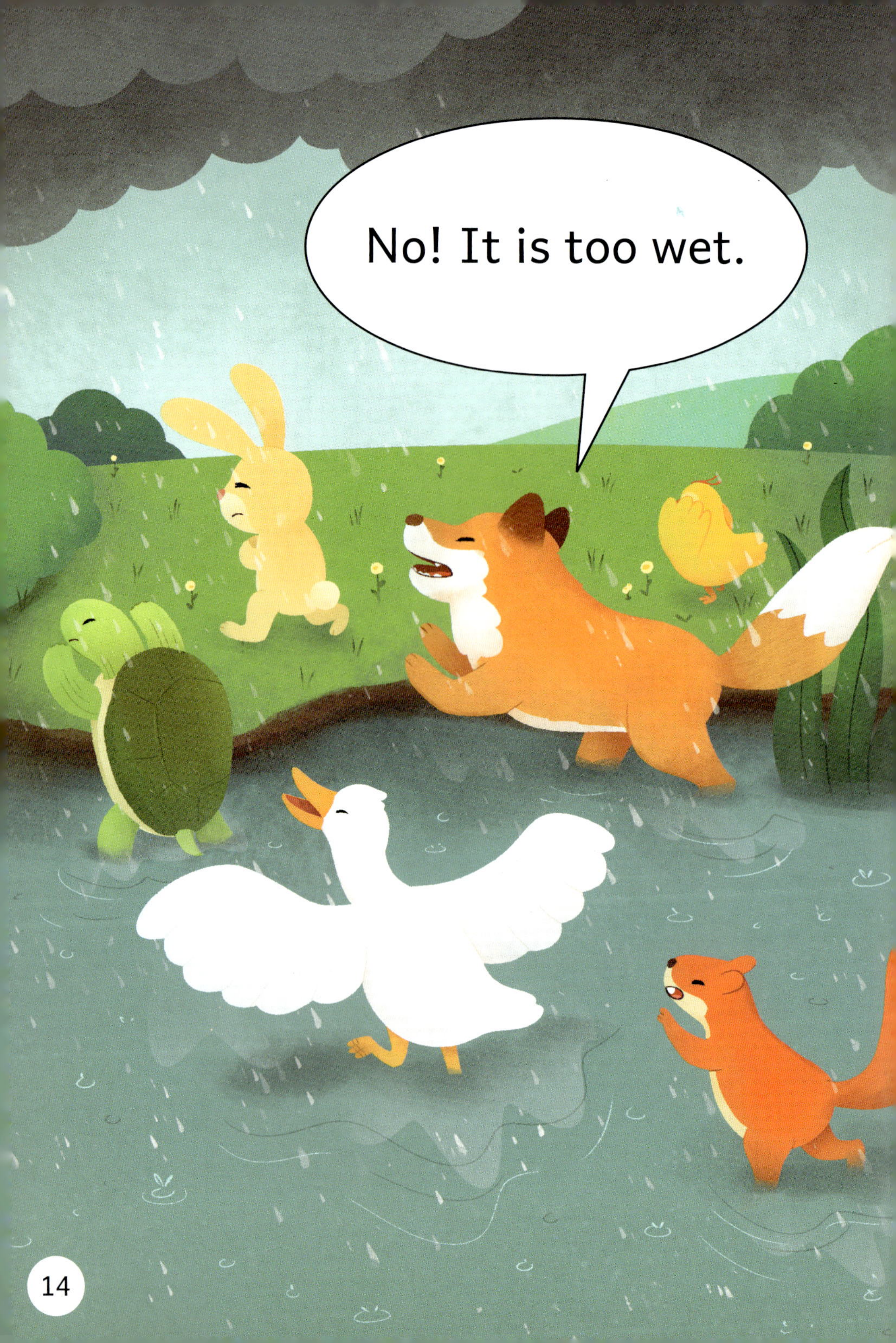
No! It is too wet.

The pond was not crowded.

"This is better," said Duck.

"Yes," said Fish.
"This is better."

The Letter W

Trace the lower and upper case letter with a finger. Sound out the letter.

*Down,
up,
down,
up*

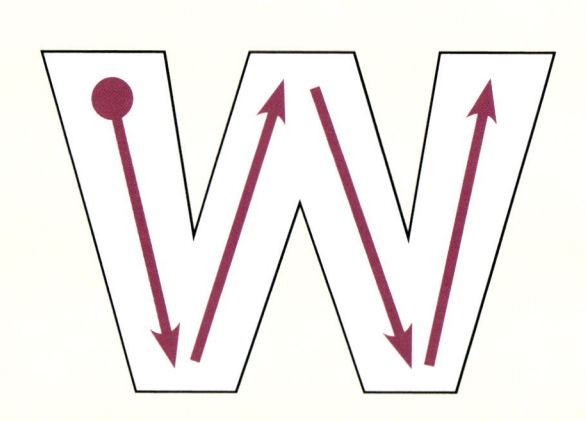

*Down,
up,
down,
up*

Some words to familiarise:

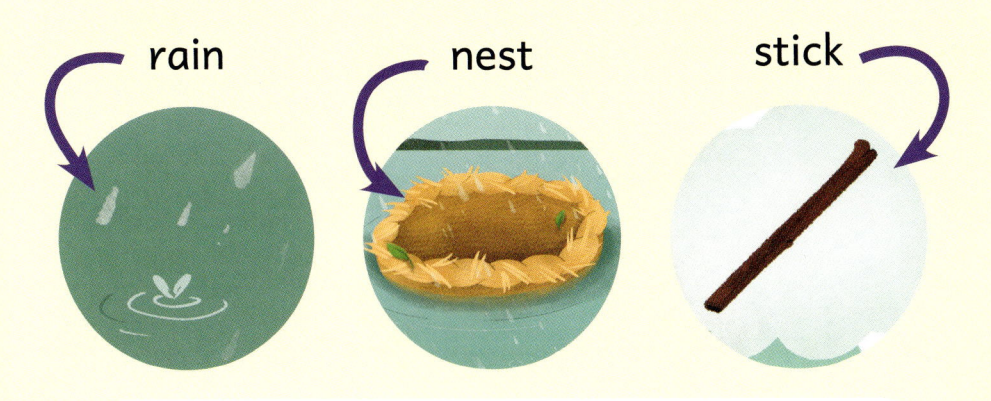

rain   nest   stick

High-frequency words:

it   was   a   the   all   is
up   said   in   you   me

Tips for Reading 'The Wet Day'

- Practise the words listed above before reading the story.
- If the reader struggles with any of the other words, ask them to look for sounds they know in the word. Encourage them to sound out the words and help them read the words if necessary.
- After reading the story, ask the reader what Duck asked Fish for.

Fun Activity

Discuss what you'd like to do if it was a rainy day!

The Wet Day

It was a wet day.

Rain fell into the pond.

Duck and Fish had fun.

The rain fell and fell.

The rain fell all day.

"The pond is filling up!" said Duck.

Duck's nest was bobbing
in the pond.

"Too much rain!" said Fish.

"Can you get me a stick?"
said Duck.

"Yes!" said Fish.

The rain fell into the pond and Duck's nest was wet.

But Duck and Fish had fun in the rain.

Book Bands for Guided Reading

Pink
Red
Yellow
Blue
Green
Orange
Turquoise
Purple
Gold
White

The Institute of Education book banding system is a scale of colours that reflects the various levels of reading difficulty. The bands are assigned by taking into account the content, the language style, the layout and phonics. Word, phrase and sentence level work is also taken into consideration.

Maverick Early Readers are a bright, attractive range of books covering the pink to white bands. All of these books have been book banded for guided reading to the industry standard and edited by a leading educational consultant.

To view the whole Maverick Readers scheme, visit our website at
www.maverickearlyreaders.com

Or scan the QR code above to view our scheme instantly!